Going Through? Walk IT Out!

Living God's Word Through Life's Trials

B. C. Raines

Going Through? Walk IT Out!

Living God's Word Through Life's Trials

CONTENTS

CONTENTS (continued)

ACKNOWLEDGMENTS

To all of those who allowed me to be myself during my
wilderness season…
Thank you!

To those who laughed at me and mocked me during my
wilderness season…
Thank you!

To those who judged me during my wilderness season…
Thank you!

For those who loved me through my wilderness season…
Thank you!

It all worked out for my good and His glory.
I am who I am today because of every experience—
the good, the bad, and the other.

Thank you to those who kept pushing me to keep writing
and get this book out of me and into your hands.

INTRODUCTION

Going Through?
Walk IT Out!
Living God's Word Through Life's Trials

"IT" in this title is two-fold: the situation and the solution.

Going through? Walk IT out! Walk it—*the situation*—out. Oftentimes when trouble comes our way, we would rather run as quickly as we can in the opposite direction and hide rather than go through the situation. These unfamiliar and uncomfortable growth moments are just a part of life, especially the life of a Christian.

Going through? Walk IT—*the Word of God* (the solution)—out. What does IT say about your situation? IT? Yes, the Word of God. It is a word meant to be lived in our everyday lives right here and now. The Word of God (IT) is full of instruction for every area of our lives. Yep, some biblical guidance is right at your fingertips.

The Word of God is flawless (Prov 30:5), meaning it's perfect. It's a promise. It's a guarantee. Whatever it says will certainly occur. It also says that His faithfulness is my armor and protection (Psalm 91:4). This means that God's faithfulness—His promise to do and be just what He said—is all I need to take the next step on my lonely journey, to get up from the blows of life that beat me down. I knew that I could depend on Him to be everything that He said He would be and do everything that He promised. I learned how to rest in Him. Just His faithfulness...

I went through a very trying time for several consecutive years in my life. There was not one area of my life that was not impacted during this time—my relationships, my health, and even my sanity. This experience, which I also refer to as my *"wilderness"* season, began in 2015 and continued through 2022. In some instances, I felt that no one understood my situation, nor did I even want to talk about it most of the time. So, I really began to see what the Word said about how I was to respond or even what to expect from the situations in my life at that time, and wow! My finds were amazing! They brought me through, which is why I want to share them with you as well. I also encourage you to search for your own gems in the Word. There are plenty of them and trust me, they will be all you need.

I experienced a lot of emotions, too, during this time. I had to learn that overcoming these emotions is a process. For me, some of these emotions resurfaced over and over and over again and each time they resurfaced, I kept applying the Word. The more I saw my situations play out the way the Word said they would, the more confident I became in God's faithfulness and promises. I encourage you to keep speaking the Word to your situation(s). There is so much in what we speak, especially during trying times.

Included in this handbook are some of the feelings and situations that I experienced during my time in the *wilderness* and the promises I found that kept me sane and helped me through it. You will notice that many times the same scripture would help me walk through different situations. I hope that these promises will help you, too!

My prayer for you:

I pray from God's glorious, unlimited resources that He will empower you with inner strength through His Spirit. I also pray that Christ will make His home in your heart as you trust Him more. May you be rooted and grounded in God's marvelous love that you may be able to understand how wide, how long, how high, and how deep His love is. May you have this understanding so that you may experience the love of Christ, which is too great to fully understand. Then you will be made complete with all the fullness of life and power that comes from God. Amen.
(Source: Ephesians 3: 16-19)

Going Through?
Walk IT Out!

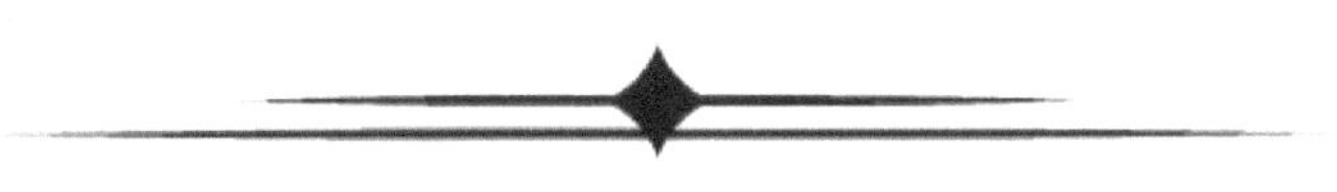

*I began to make God's standard my standard
and it took the pressure off me
to always please everybody.*

Acceptance

The need for acceptance is something that I struggled with for many years. I was raised to not *need* anyone to do anything in life. One of my mom's favorite sayings was, *"You came into this world by yourself and you will leave by yourself."* In essence, you came alone into this world and you'll leave alone. Therefore, don't depend on anyone while you live life between your coming and going.

In theory, this is a good approach when training your children to not yield to peer pressure or do something simply because everybody is doing it--but there is a basic human need for acceptance. We all, at some point in our lives, want to be accepted by our peers, and most times we want to find a special someone for companionship and love.

Well, the fulfillment of those needs didn't chase me down and overtake me. I generally was not approached for dates, and even most of my friendships did not last over time. It wasn't until I learned and accepted that Jesus had already accepted me and that was enough. This realization stopped my yearning so much to be accepted by others. When I embraced this fact, I no longer had to morph into being what others expected because I wanted to be accepted by people. I began to make God's standard my standard and it took the pressure off me to always please everybody.

***IT, the Word, says:**
Psalm 139:14 NIV
I praise you because I am fearfully and wonderfully
made; your works are wonderful, I know that full well.*

*__Romans 15:7 NIV__
Accept one another, then, just as Christ accepted you, in
order to bring praise to God.*

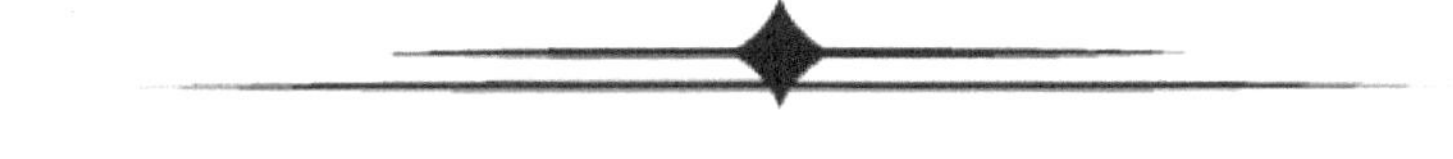

Anger is a natural and normal emotion. Feeling anger is not bad.
It's how we handle the anger that colors it good or bad. Anger can work for us or against us.

Anger

I was very angry with so many people during my *wilderness* season, but more than anything, I was angry with myself. I was not supposed to be in a situation like this at this point in my life. Not allowing my anger to fester was a daily struggle. I even became angry with God because I didn't understand why He chose to allow things to unfold the way they did. You see, I had prayed and prayed and prayed. I had asked Him to disrupt my actions if they were not in line with His perfect will for me. But He didn't. I'll tell you, anger probably doesn't even begin to describe how I felt sometimes.

Anger is a natural and normal emotion. Feeling anger is not bad. It's how we handle the anger that colors it good or bad. However, anger must be handled. It festers and creates a big mess if it isn't. I commonly compare it to red sauce cooking on the stovetop. If that sauce goes unattended for too long, it will eventually boil over and there will be splatters of red sauce EVERYWHERE! On the stove, the walls, the floor, and even the ceiling. Splatters will be in places that you will discover long after the initial clean-up. Deal with the anger. Control your anger. Don't let your anger control you!

Here is what IT—the Word—says about anger:

Proverbs 19:11 NLT
Sensible people control their temper; they earn respect by overlooking wrongs.

Ephesians 4:26-27 NLT
[26] And "don't sin by letting anger control you."[a] Don't let the sun go down while you are still angry, [27] for anger gives a foothold to the devil.

James 1:19-20 NIV
[19] My dear brothers and sisters, take note of this: Everyone should be quick to listen, slow to speak and slow to become angry, [20] because human anger does not produce the righteousness that God desires.

*The one thing that has helped me quiet my anxiety is
that I already know everything
will work out for my good and His glory.*

Anxiety/Worry

Anxiety. That constant unresolved feeling that is keeping you focused on the what ifs. Anxiety can rob you of your present and future. It keeps you unsettled and unfocused. You become a walking nervous wreck.

The one thing that has helped me quiet my anxiety is that I already know everything will work out for my good and His glory. (Remember His faithfulness is our armor and protection.) When I plant my emotions on this simple truth, I get some solid footing under me as I navigate those rocky uncertain spots on the journey.

Here's what IT— the Word—reminds us about anxiety/worry:

Philippians 4:6 NIV

Do not be anxious about anything, but in every situation, by prayer and petition, with thanksgiving, present your requests to God.

Are you feeling some anxiety about anything in your life? Here's your answer: pray, give thanks, and present your requests to God. We know that when we pray in line with God's will, He not only hears us, but He is also certain to answer.

1John 5: 14-15 NLT

[14] And we are confident that he hears us whenever we ask for anything that pleases him. [15] And since we know he

hears us when we make our requests, we also know that he will give us what we ask for.

Why worry about anything? If God takes care of the birds of the air and the flowers in the field, why doubt if He will take care of you? Put Him first and He promises that you will have everything that you need.

Matthew 6:25-34 NIV

"Therefore I tell you, do not worry about your life, what you will eat or drink; or about your body, what you will wear. Is not life more than food, and the body more than clothes? [26] Look at the birds of the air; they do not sow or reap or store away in barns, and yet your heavenly Father feeds them. Are you not much more valuable than they? [27] Can any one of you by worrying add a single hour to your life? [28] "And why do you worry about clothes? See how the flowers of the field grow. They do not labor or spin. [29] Yet I tell you that not even Solomon in all his splendor was dressed like one of these. [30] If that is how God clothes the grass of the field, which is here today and tomorrow is thrown into the fire, will he not much more clothe you—you of little faith? [31] So do not worry, saying, 'What shall we eat?' or 'What shall we drink?' or 'What shall we wear?' [32] For the pagans run after all these things, and your heavenly Father knows that you need them. [33] But seek first his kingdom and his righteousness, and all these things will be given to you as well. [34] Therefore do not worry about tomorrow, for tomorrow will worry about itself. Each day has enough trouble of its own.

Betrayal doesn't surprise God.
Jesus experienced betrayal from within His very inner circle—His disciples—
the ones He handpicked to accompany Him on this Earth.

Betrayal

Betrayal hurts. And the closer the person is to you and your heart, the harsher the betrayal feels. It can be a blow to your very soul. You know for most of us, there are just certain people in our lives that we KNOW will never betray us. So, when it happens (I know for me), the disbelief is unreal. It shook the very foundations of my being and made me analyze every relationship that I had with everybody. After a betrayal of that magnitude, I think I honestly stopped expecting total loyalty from anyone.

Betrayal doesn't surprise God. Jesus experienced betrayal from within His very inner circle—His disciples--the ones He handpicked to accompany Him on this Earth.
Honestly, what got me through the betrayal was knowing what IT said about what would happen to those who betrayed me.

IT says:

Proverbs 26: 27 NIV
Whoever digs a pit will fall into it; if someone rolls a stone, it will roll back on them.

Psalm 35:4-8 NIV
⁴ May those who seek my life be disgraced and put to shame;
may those who plot my ruin be turned back in dismay.
⁵ May they be like chaff before the wind, with the angel of

the Lord driving them away; ⁶ may their path be dark and slippery, with the angel of the Lord pursuing them.⁷ Since they hid their net for me without cause and without cause dug a pit for me, ⁸ may ruin overtake them by surprise— may the net they hid entangle them, may they fall into the pit, to their ruin.

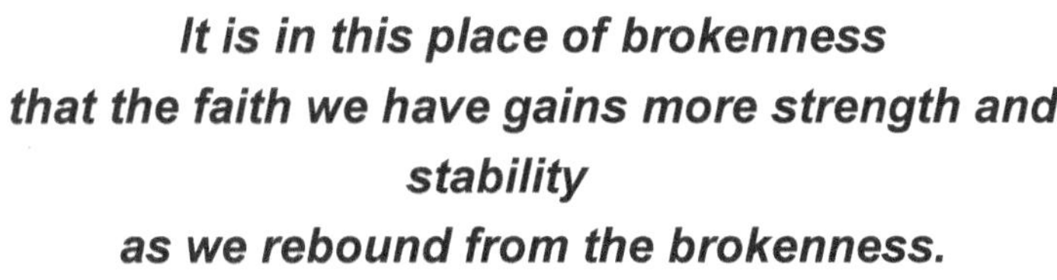

*It is in this place of brokenness
that the faith we have gains more strength and
stability
as we rebound from the brokenness.*

Brokenness

Shattered. Gut punched. Fragmented. Crushed. Shards.

How do I recover from this? What just happened? Am I in a nightmare? Ain't no way to get over this one. Yes, I've been to all those places. Sometimes, all at once.

It's that blow that knocked me to my knees and while I was on my knees, the next one came, and the blows kept coming and eventually laid me out. But I thought to myself: if it doesn't kill me, I will recover from even this. And because of this brokenness, I'll come back stronger than I was when I got knocked down. It is in this place of brokenness that the faith we have gains more strength and stability as we rebound from the brokenness.

My favorite mantra: This won't break me; it will make me!

IT says:

Psalm 34:18 NLT
The Lord is close to the brokenhearted; he rescues those whose spirits are crushed.

Proverbs 24:16 NIV
For though the righteous fall seven times, they rise again, but the wicked stumble when calamity strikes.

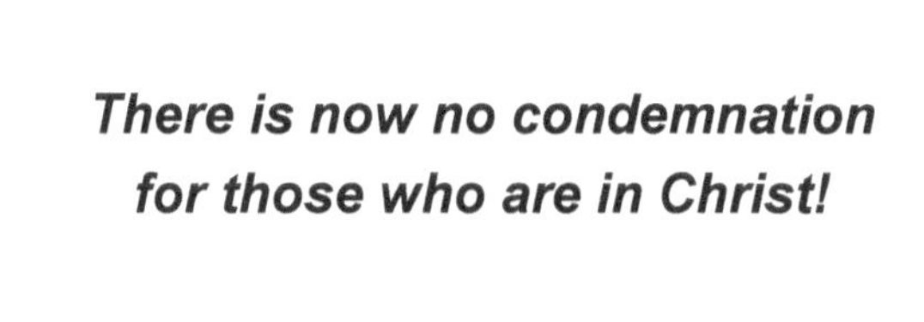

There is now no condemnation
for those who are in Christ!

Condemnation

How could you be so stupid? You won't ever learn. You're such an idiot, such a disappointment to yourself and your family. I said these statements about myself to myself for a while during my wilderness. I said them so much that I actually started to believe them.

Here's an online dictionary's definition of condemnation:
1.the expression of very strong disapproval; censure: "there was strong international condemnation of the attack" synonyms: censure · criticism · strictures · denunciation · vilification · reproof.
2.the action of condemning someone to a punishment; sentencing.

When we say these types of statements to ourselves, (like those I was saying to myself), we are in essence inflicting a punishment on ourselves.

Now here's what IT, the Word, says about condemnation:

Romans 8:1-2 NIV
Therefore, there is now no condemnation for those who are in Christ Jesus, [2] because through Christ Jesus the law of the Spirit who gives life has set you free from the law of sin and death.

God is not the author of confusion.

Confusion

God is not the author of confusion. If there is any confusion in a situation just know that God didn't cause the confusion. That is the enemy all day long.

So, how do we handle confusion? Separating ourselves from the confusion is great if this is a viable option. Creating some space from the situation will allow us to access what's really going on. It will also give us a physical and mental break from the situation.

During these times of confusion, if you don't seem to hear from God, just stand still until you do. Don't move to the left or the right. Don't move backward or forward. Even if someone you know and trust tells you which way to move, do not move. Just stand still. Don't move until you hear from God about what to do and which way to go. Yes, God may send a sign of confirmation through someone else, but He would have given His direction first. The sign comes after the directions. The confusion is designed to distract you from hearing God.

IT says:

John 10:27 KJV
My sheep hear my voice, and I know them, and they follow me…

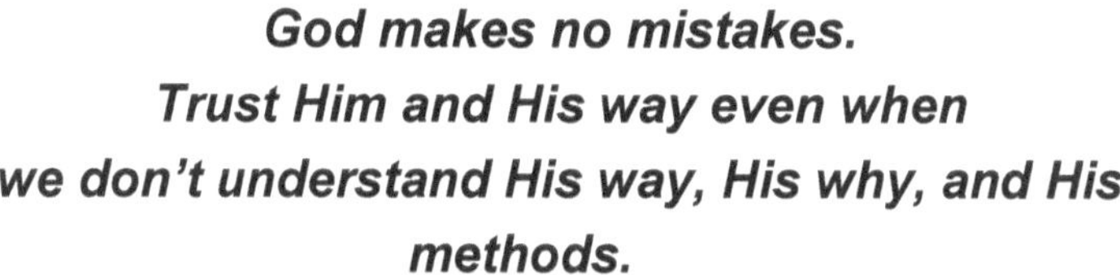

God makes no mistakes.
Trust Him and His way even when
we don't understand His way, His why, and His
methods.

Death of Loved One

2020 was a year of death for so many. COVID-19 shut down the world and people were dying by the thousands. COVID seemed to not have any rhyme or reason about how it struck, who it struck, and who died as a result. It was a scary time for most. There was so much uncertainty. My family and I were not immune to these deaths. In November 2022, my church father died as a result of COVID complications. In early 2021, a dear church member from my home church also died from COVID complications. These deaths hurt but they weren't knockouts for me like so many faced by others. COVID was killing multiple generations within families.

My gut-kicking deaths started in 2021. First was my uncle, my aunt's husband. He died in February 2021. He had been sick for a long time and his death was somewhat anticipated but still, we weren't prepared. My aunt, my mom's only sister, had passed in the 1990s and this uncle never remarried. I spent a lot of time with my uncle, aunt, and cousins as a young child, so his death was like closing a chapter to my early childhood. It was also devastating for my mom because in some way he was the last link to her sister and their younger days together.

Then, my young cousin passed away on July 17, 2021. He was the youngest child of the uncle who had passed away in February of the same year. In my mind, I always referred to him as my little cousin—he was the youngest of his siblings.

I had my own special connection with him. He definitely had a special place in my heart. I was like a big sister he never had. His death was not expected. He went to the hospital and was improving on a daily basis, talking about all that he was going to do when he got home from the hospital. He never returned home. Talk about a shocker…

While reeling from this sudden loss of my cousin, I learned a few days later- on social media, of all places- that a dear friend of mine had been murdered. Her murder occurred on the 20th of July. MURDERED! Who does this? Who does this to a friend of mine? My friends don't get murdered! Her youngest son is the same age as my son. We would celebrate their November birthdays together. What in the world?

My cousin's funeral and my friend's memorial were held on the same day. I couldn't fully support either family. I was torn and tired. The best I could be was present and in the moment while trying to deal with my own emotions and feelings.

June 29, 2022…the death of my mom. Her death was bittersweet. My mom had fought numerous auto-immune and connective tissue diseases for years and she always bounced back from the crises. ALWAYS! However, I knew this time was different. The hospital stays were longer and more frequent. Mom was tired and she voiced it more than she had ever before. This went on for about a year. The last six weeks of life were the most miserable for her. She was bedridden and couldn't do anything for herself. She couldn't use her limbs.

As her daughter, I felt helpless because there was not much I could do to alleviate her misery. I tried to comfort her in any way that I could but as her time here on Earth dwindled, even those "magic tricks" stopped working. As I stated, her death was bittersweet. Bitter because she's gone but sweet because she's no longer miserable and suffering. Man, I miss my mom!

NOTE: Make sure that your loved ones are saved. Don't assume that because they grew up in church or attend church frequently, that they are saved. Church attendance does not equal salvation. I know this can be an uncomfortable conversation to approach but one that is VERY necessary. It brings so much comfort to you when you know that your loved is saved. As my Pastor mentioned, it also takes their mind off of the death to come.

God makes no mistakes. Trust Him and His way even when we don't understand His way, His why, and His methods.

The IT promises that got me through:

2 Samuel 22:31 NIV and NLT
*As for **God**, his way is perfect; the word of the LORD is perfect: He is a shield for all who look to him for protection.*

Psalm 30:5 NKJV

...Weeping may endure for a night, But joy comes in the morning.

Psalm 34:18 NLT

The Lord is close to the brokenhearted; he rescues those whose spirits are crushed.

Psalm 147:3 NLT

He heals the brokenhearted and bandages their wounds.

2 Corinthians 5: 6-8 NKJV

[6] So we are always confident, knowing that while we are at home in the body we are absent from the Lord. [7] For we walk by faith, not by sight. [8] We are confident, yes, well pleased rather to be absent from the body and to be present with the Lord.

Salvation scripture:

Romans 10: 9-10 NIV

[9] If you declare with your mouth, "Jesus is Lord," and believe in your heart that God raised him from the dead, you will be saved. [10] For it is with your heart that you believe and are justified, and it is with your mouth that you profess your faith and are saved.

Ask your loved one: Do you believe in your heart that God raised Jesus from the dead? If they offer affirmation verbally or with a gesture, then they are saved.

Typically, I don't get fairy tale endings.

Disappointment

Disappointment. Disbelief. Disgust. I could go on and on listing words that describe what disappointment feels like--- and I am sure you can too.

I have experienced so much disappointment. For me, disappointment makes it hard to be excited about life. Typically, I don't get fairy tale endings. Even when I've allowed myself to get excited about an anticipated happy ending, it always seems to be the exact opposite of what I expected.

My life adjustment has been to not expect too much from other people or situations. Instead, I just navigate gracefully through whatever situations I face. I really don't make a big deal out of events or milestones in my life and that way, I avoid being disappointed. That sounds like a dreadful life, right? Yes, I know. I'm working on it.

Here's how IT is helping me walk through the disappointment:

Proverbs 13:12 NKJV
Hope deferred makes the heart sick, But when the desire comes, it is a tree of life.

Proverb 15:13 NIV
A happy heart makes the face cheerful, but heartache crushes the spirit.

It occurred to me that I didn't have to strategize because a double-minded person is unstable in ALL their ways.

Double-Mindedness

So, I found myself dealing with a few people who were saying one thing to my face and something else behind my back. The two of them were speaking with me individually, but they were both discussing me with each other - and anyone else who would listen. The talk was very different when they weren't in my presence.

Initially, I was anxious. I saw the potential traps and was trying to think through my strategy for how to respond. (To better help you understand my need to strategize, you must understand that where I grew up, backbiting and being two-faced could get you into a serious fight. Like an "as-soon-as-we-get-off-this-bus" kind of fight. These behaviors were not tolerated in my neighborhood and folks dealt with the "guilty party" immediately.)

Then, I remembered what IT says in James 1:8: *"A double-minded man is unstable in all his ways."* Immediately, I began to search the Word for guidance on how to respond to these encounters. It occurred to me that I didn't have to strategize because a double-minded person is unstable in ALL their ways. So, if this is the behavior you are exhibiting towards me, then it's the behavior that you are exhibiting with others as well. Eventually, all of the back biting and two-facedness will be exposed and consequences will follow-- consequences that only God can allow or arrange. WHEW! Fellow believer, just keep moving forward ethically, with integrity, and with the goal of pleasing Him even in this…everything will be okay.

My IT treasures:

Exodus 14:14 NIV
The Lord will fight for you. You need only to be still. (This one, I made personal: "The Lord will fight for me. I need only to be still." I speak this scripture daily over my life.)

Proverbs 16:7 NKJV
When a man's ways please the LORD, he maketh even his enemies to be at peace with him.

Proverbs 26:24-27 NIV
Enemies disguise themselves with their lips, but in their hearts they harbor deceit. [25] Though their speech is charming, do not believe them, for seven abominations fill their hearts. [26] Their malice may be concealed by deception, but their wickedness will be exposed in the assembly. [27] Whoever digs a pit will fall into it; if someone rolls a stone, it will roll back on them.

Colossians 3:23 NKJV
Whatever you do, do your work heartily, as for the Lord rather than for men;

James 1:8 KJV
A double-minded man is unstable in all his ways.

*But I promise you that if God has asked you to do something,
He will provide everything you need to
accomplish the assignment and its related tasks.*

Fear

False **E**vidence **A**ppearing **R**eal. I read this acrostic once many years ago and it stuck with me. (I don't remember the author.) Fear is the one thing that can stifle us in ways that we may not even realize. It's the "what-ifs" about the unknown. It's telling yourself that it didn't work the last time and so I better even not try it this time. "Ain't nobody ever did this before, so I'd better use common sense and not do it either".

Like anger, fear is not always bad. Sometimes we need to pay attention to fear because it can be an internal signal to us that something is not right. When we allow our fear to stifle us, to discourage us, it can keep us from going where we want to go in life.

What IT says:

Joshua 1:9 NIV
Have I not commanded you? Be strong and courageous. Do not be afraid; do not be discouraged, for the Lord your God will be with you wherever you go."

Psalm 34:4 NIV
I sought the Lord, and he answered me; he delivered me from all my fears.

Most times the assignments from God may seem much bigger than we are. In many instances, the tasks require more than our available resources and the fear arises. We may even begin to question if, in fact, this is really even God talking to us. But I promise you that if God has asked you to do something, He will provide everything you need to accomplish the assignment and its related tasks. These are faith-building moments in our lives. Remember, His thoughts are not our thoughts, His ways are not our ways and we should not lean on our own understanding.

IT says:

Deceptive flattery can alter relationships, create distance, and erode trust.

Flattery

I got hurt a lot by the use of flattery. I had some people in my life who used this tool in a deceptive way quite often, but I had no clue. For most of my life, I had known these specific people to be very truthful, so to learn that they had told me what they thought I wanted to hear instead of what was true–crushed me. Hearing those words devastated me on levels that I did not even know existed within me.

Prior to this wilderness season, I thought that flattery was telling someone that the dress they wore was pretty when I knew that I didn't like it. But that compliment surely made the other person feel good, so what was the harm?

The use of flattery can be very deceptive. Yes, our words may sound good coming out of our mouths but if those words are not honest or are used to deceive, they can be devastating, especially to the person hearing them. Don't compliment me when you know what you are saying is not true. Don't give me advice that you know is not good or wise advice.

Deceptive flattery can alter relationships, create distance, and erode trust. Those once-trusted relationships are forever changed. When you know someone isn't being truthful and honest, it's hard to trust what they say. The person using the flattery may feel "some kind of way" after seeing that there is now distance in the relationship. Deceptive flattery doesn't do anyone any good!

Now, honesty is always the best way, but it is not a license to be insulting and degrading to other people. As my mom used to say, *"If you can't say something nice, don't say anything at all"*. Keep the insults to yourself. Speak the truth out of a place of love and always be kind regardless of what you say. Most times, it's not what you say--it's how you say it that leaves the most lasting impression.

What IT says:

Proverb 26:28 NIV
A lying tongue hates those it hurts, and a flattering mouth works ruin.

Proverbs 29:5 NIV
Those who flatter their neighbors are spreading nets for their feet.

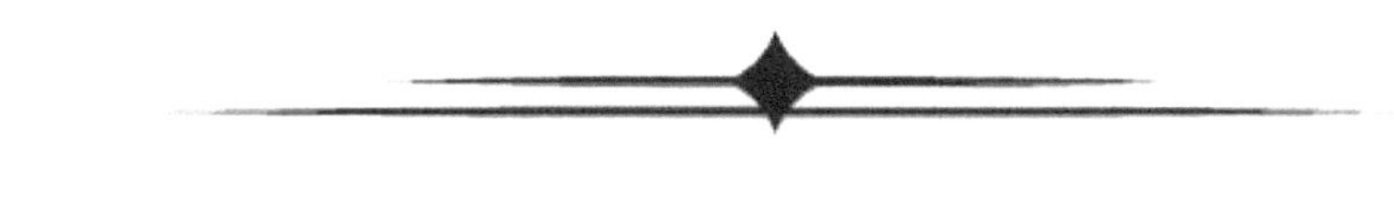

Grief is a process that can be triggered by any loss.

Grief

Grief is a process that can be triggered by any loss. ANY LOSS. A loss can be the end of a relationship through any means—death, divorce, or just the relationship ending without knowing or accepting the reason why. A loss could be losing a home due to foreclosure, a devasting fire, or a natural disaster. A loss can also be termination from a job. ANY loss can cause grief.

The thing about grief is that how we handle it looks different for everybody. Some laugh. Some cry. Some drink. Some eat. Some work. Some talk. Some don't. Some sleep. Some ignore their feelings about their loss. As for me, I sometimes have this uncontrollable urge to just cry at very random moments. Sometimes I can explain why I want to cry. Other times, I can't.

I am a giver, so during the times when I'm struggling the most, I try to do something nice for someone else. For instance, on the one-year observation of my mom's passing, I celebrated the birthdays of some people whose birthdays fell on my mom's death date. I even coined the date as her HBD—Heaven Bound Date. I used the same common abbreviation for Happy Birthday. It allowed me to reflect on life and not so much on death. (It's different—I know. But it was a healthy way for me to observe a significant and difficult day in my life.)

Grieving is a natural response to experiencing loss. The important thing to remember about grief is that there is help if you're going through IT!

59

IT says:

Psalm 30:5 NKJV
Weeping may endure for a night, But joy comes in the morning.

Matthew 5:4 NIV
Blessed are those who mourn, for they will be comforted.

*"God has already forgiven you.
Now tell them that's all that matters".*

Guilt/Regret

Guilt. Regret. I wallowed in those for a while. Others helped me stay in my pity party of guilt and regret as well. Yes, I made some mistakes that I should have known better than to make in this stage of my life. How did I get here? How did I get this far gone? Why didn't I see the signs? I felt so stupid!

As I struggled with forgiving myself, there were people in my immediate circle who constantly reminded me of my mistakes. Those reminders quickly sent me into a tailspin of negative thoughts and emotions. What really helped me to deal with their words was something that my Pastor said one Sunday during service: *"God has already forgiven you. Now tell them that's all that matters."* I think he also said to tell them, *"Now you take it up with God."* (If he didn't, I heard it from somewhere, and I certainly used it when needed.) I was really able to communicate these words in my defense when the attacks came. This was a game-changer.

This is the condemnation that I talked about in an earlier chapter. It's the constant belittling by others – or that you do to yourself – that depletes your every hope that things will get better. It's the constant replaying of what you should have said or what you should have done to avoid the unpleasant consequences that you are currently facing. It feels like a constant black cloud that follows only you. The condemnation was hard to break. I had to keep telling myself that condemnation was not of God. It got easier once I no longer gave others permission to voice, to me, their condemnation of me.

IT says:

Romans 8:1
NIV Therefore, there is now no condemnation for those who are in Christ Jesus,

MSG *1-2 With the arrival of Jesus, the Messiah, that fateful dilemma is resolved. Those who enter into Christ's being here for us no longer have to live under a continuous, low-lying black cloud. A new power is in operation. The Spirit of life in Christ, like a strong wind, has magnificently cleared the air, freeing you from a fated lifetime of brutal tyranny at the hands of sin and death.*

Another lesson learned about guilt and regret: God can use any situation. Nothing changes His plan for our lives. Just trust that even this situation can be used to carry out the plan. He is masterful in incorporating these regrettable moments into the wonderful picture of your life. He can…
massage an awesome message out of the mess;
verse a vast victory for the victim; and
tender a tenacious testimony from the test.
He's that kind of God!

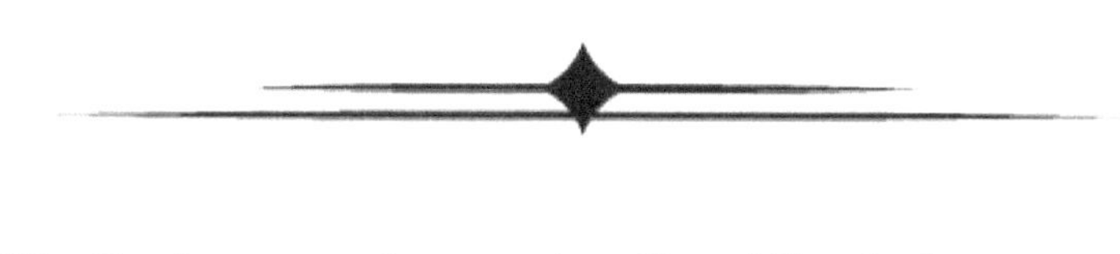

My God yearns for me to allow Him to be my everything.

I'm Alone/Abandoned

We are never alone! Our God is always with us!

I had to keep reminding myself of this very truth so many times. Sometimes, I just want to have a physical person that I can talk to and confide in. Sometimes, I just want others to be as available to me as I am to them. Sometimes, I just want folks to be loyal, trustworthy, and dependable. You know…be the person that follows through on their promises. Be the person that honors our relationship enough to be committed to me even on my worst days.

Abandonment…man! I didn't realize it then but as I matured, I realized that abandonment had been very present in my life as a young and developing child. What I learned was that I could not depend on anybody and all I had to rely on was me, myself, and I. Boy, was I wrong. I was not designed to live this life on my own. My God yearns for me to allow Him to be my everything.

IT says:

Deuteronomy 31:6 NLT
Be strong and courageous. Do not be afraid or terrified because of them, for the LORD your God goes with you; he will never leave you nor forsake you."

Deuteronomy 31:8 NIV

*The LORD himself goes before **you** and will be with **you**; he will never leave **you** nor **forsake you**. Do **not** be afraid; do **not** be discouraged."*

Psalm 118:7a NIV

The Lord is with me; He is my helper.

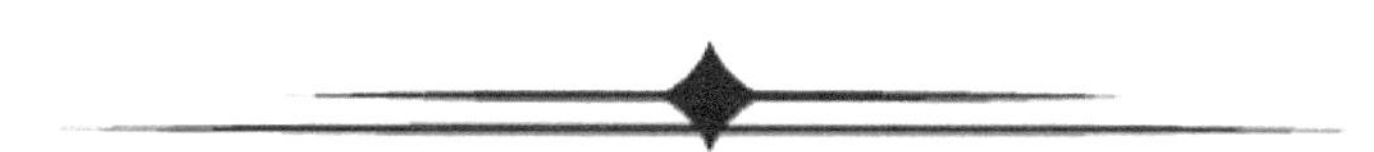

*I believe that God will allow more than we can
humanly bear because
that's when we are most likely to search for His help.*

Overwhelmed

This is too much for me! Bills are due but there is no money to pay them. Folks on my job are talking about me behind my back and sabotaging my name. I am sick in my body--I just don't feel well and can't seem to get better. Everywhere I turn, someone close to me is dying. I can't seem to catch a break. Nothing seems to be working in my favor. I don't know what else to do, which way to turn, or where to go! I'm sick and tired of being sick and tired; just frustrated…exhausted! Whew…just overwhelmed!

I have often heard it said that God won't give us any more than we can bear. After my wilderness season, I don't agree with this statement (nor have I been able to find this promise in the Word. I'm not disputing that it's there, I just haven't found it). I believe that God will allow more than we can humanly bear because that's when we are most likely to search for His help. This is the way He intended us to live all along—dependent on Him.

So, here's what I found to help me when I am feeling overwhelmed with the things in my life that seem unbearable and just way too much…

IT says:

2 Chronicles 16:9 ERV
The eyes of the LORD go around looking in all the earth for people who are faithful to him so that he can make them strong.

Psalm 14:2 NIV
The LORD looks down from heaven to see if there is anyone who is wise, anyone who looks to him for help.

Psalm 118:13 MSG
I was right on the cliff-edge, ready to fall, when God grabbed and held me.

Vengeance belongs to God and not to me.

Revenge

During my wilderness season, my thoughts of revenge were mostly plotting how to expose the character of the ones that were hurting me. I was so hurt, and the hurt kept coming. I wanted folks to know that "so-and-so" was a liar. I wanted everybody to know that in many instances, I was the victim and not the aggressor or the initiator. I just wanted people to know the truth—not the lies that had been spewed about me. So many lies had been told about me. I had not done anything to these people. In fact, I had in most instances been very kind and generous to the initiators. I just wanted to clear my name and was willing to expose others to get the truth out. But God…

I kept remembering what IT—the Word of God—says: "Vengeance is mine…" Vengeance belongs to God and not to me. One thing that I have learned over time is it's best to allow their Creator (our God) to exact revenge or consequences, because who knows better about what will really impact the person? Their Creator knows them best and knows just what it will take to get their attention. You see, from God's perspective, it's not about me. He will use every opportunity to remind His children to return to Him.

My IT reminders:

Proverb 17: 13 NIV
*Evil will never leave the house of one who pays back evil
for good.*

Isaiah 54:17 NLT
*But in that coming day no weapon turned against you will
succeed.
You will silence every voice raised up to accuse you.
These benefits are enjoyed by the servants of
the Lord; their vindication will come from me. I, the Lord,
have spoken!*

Romans 12:19
KJV *Dearly beloved, avenge not yourselves, but rather
give place unto wrath: for it is written, Vengeance is mine; I
will repay, saith the Lord.*

NLT *Dear friends, never take revenge. Leave that to the
righteous anger of God. For the Scriptures say, "I will take
revenge; I will pay them back, says the Lord.*

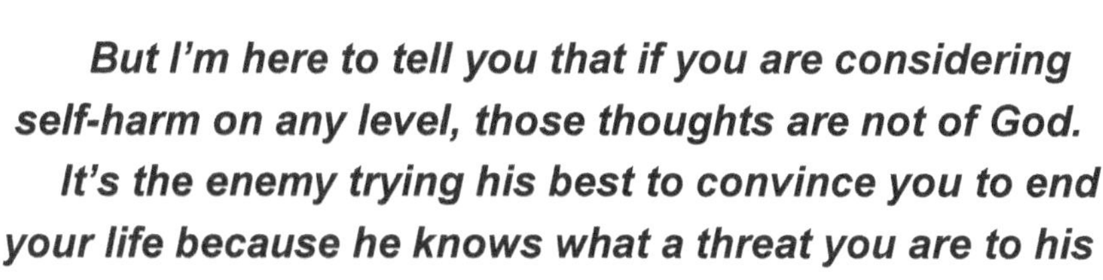

But I'm here to tell you that if you are considering self-harm on any level, those thoughts are not of God. It's the enemy trying his best to convince you to end your life because he knows what a threat you are to his agenda.

Self-harm Thoughts

Suicidal thoughts are not talked about in church. My mom used to say that when a person commits suicide, they automatically go to hell because they didn't have a chance to repent. Most of us have been taught to be ashamed of these thoughts and to deny that they even exist. However, Christians deal with these thoughts more than anyone would care to imagine.

Yes, I'll admit it: there were many times that I thought about ending my own life. The time I remember most vividly is the morning of my 47th birthday. I actually woke up thinking about where I could hang myself. I had already mentally exhausted the other viable options. I didn't have enough of any kind of drugs on which to overdose. I did not own a gun, nor did I know how to shoot a gun.

I was just mentally tired. I was physically drained. I was embarrassed. I was ashamed. I felt alone. I didn't care about my future or anyone else's. I was depressed. Life just didn't feel worth living anymore. I was sick of life and all its disappointments, upsets, pits, traps, dungeons, and harshness. I was just sick and tired of it all!

But I'm here to tell you that if you are considering self-harm on any level, those thoughts are not of God. It's the enemy trying his best to convince you to end your life because he knows what a threat you are to his agenda. If you weren't much of a threat, he wouldn't be fighting you so hard. He knows just how much influence you will have on those you encounter, the world, and God's kingdom.

Here's what IT has to say:

Jeremiah 29:11 NIV
For I know the plans I have for you," declares the Lord, "plans to prosper you and not to harm you, plans to give you hope and a future.

Psalm 138:8 EVS
The Lord will fulfil his purpose, for me.

Psalm 139:16 NIV
Your eyes saw my unformed body; all the days ordained for me were written in your book before one of them came to be.

1Corinthians 3:16-17 MSG
You realize, don't you, that you are the temple of God, and God himself is present in you? No one will get by with vandalizing God's temple, you can be sure of that. God's temple is sacred—and you, remember, are the temple.

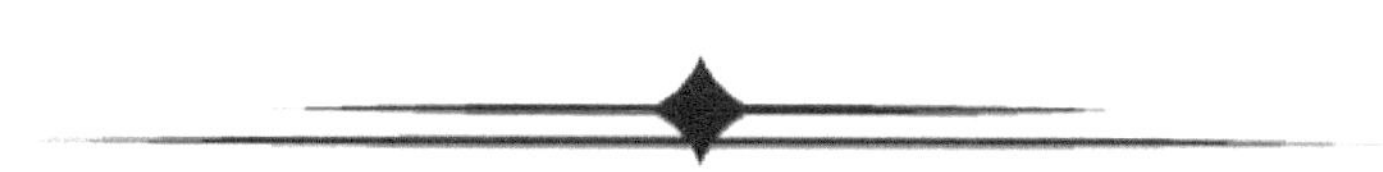

The shame of it all…
I didn't want them to know the situation I had put myself in.

Shame

Umm…the shame of it all. Due to some bad choices I made, the consequences were having a domino-like effect. I had no idea that the consequences would be like this. I knew that all that was happening was triggered by my choices and I was SO ashamed!

I didn't want anyone to know what I had done. I didn't want them to know the situation I had put myself in. I had really messed up this time. So often, I wished that I could just disappear; go someplace far, far, far away. How could I show my face around town? How could I show my face at work? Church? Around my family? I have to admit that I still deal with this one periodically. It's not as bad now as it was when I initially entered into my wilderness season, but it still lingers.

Even though I still deal with the shame, I have learned some valuable life lessons. I learned that even the ones who love us dearly can make mistakes and those mistakes can sometimes hurt us in the deepest places of our hearts. But that doesn't change their love for us, they just simply made a mistake.

I've learned that, for as long as I live, I will also make mistakes. However, when I make mistakes, I am not the mistake. I am not a failure. I simply made a mistake. I have to forgive myself and keep moving forward while discovering the lessons learned and applying them. I tell young people all the time that mistakes are absolutely going to happen. Just accept that. It's the steps after the mistake that really matter most.

IT says:

Psalm 34:4-5 NIV
[4] I sought the Lord, and he answered me; he delivered me from all my fears. [5] Those who look to him are radiant; their faces are never covered with shame.

Romans 10:11 NKJV
[11] For the Scripture says, "Whoever believes on Him will not be put to shame."

I have literally cried out to God asking that He grant me sweet sleep.
It works!

Sleepless Nights

Now, I experienced a whole lot of these—sleepless nights. I even had nights of disrupted sleep. I would fall off to sleep and then wake up again. Sometimes it was due to nightmares. Other times, I was recalling the decisions that had led to my downfall. An acquaintance of mine shared the Proverbs 3:24 scripture with me and I have to tell you, it lulled me right to sleep or back to sleep when my sleep was disrupted. I have continued to use this scripture over time so I can sleep when I find it difficult to rest my mind. I have literally cried out to God asking that He grant me sweet sleep. It works!

Rest is essential to our recovery from any trauma or life disruption. Without the proper amount of rest, our bodies and minds cannot function at their designed capacity.

IT says:

Psalm 127: 2 NIV
In vain you rise early and stay up late, toiling for food to eat—
for he grants sleep to those he loves.

Proverbs 3:24 NIV
When you lie down, you will not be afraid; when you lie down, your sleep will be sweet.

*I kept telling myself that
"by Your stripes I AM healed".*

*I knew that regardless of the outcome,
I would be okay.*

Sickness

I am one of those walking medical anomalies associated with the COVID-19 virus. Initially, my symptoms were mild and cold-like. I stayed in quarantine for the prescribed amount of time and then I returned to work. By the end of my first day back on the job, I was exhausted and felt like all of my energy and my very life had been drained out of me. I had a relenting cough and just felt awful.

This turned into multiple doctors' visits, testing, a barrage of medications, and even daily breathing treatments by machine. I wasn't able to work full days for months. Overnight, I went from walking ninety minutes a day for exercise to not being able to walk for eight consecutive minutes. It was rough. My symptoms lingered for more than a year. There was never a medical reason discovered for all of the symptoms. It even baffled the specialists.

I didn't get anxious about this health situation. (There was so much going on in my life at this time, I was just numb.) I kept telling myself that *"by Your stripes I AM healed"*. I knew that regardless of the outcome, I would be okay. If I returned to normal, I would be okay. If I developed lifelong health issues, I would be okay. If I had to leave my job, I would be okay.

Although not quite one hundred percent, I am much better than I was.

The scriptures that got me through:

Isaiah 53:5 NKJV

… and with his stripes we are healed.

Psalm 91:3 NLT

For he will rescue you from every trap and protect you from deadly disease.

Well, if the Word assures us that we will be delivered from trouble,

umm…

I think that means that we will in fact have trouble.

Trouble/Trials/Tribulations

You know, as Christians, we should expect trouble. I was amazed at how many times IT (the Word) talks about the righteous being rescued from trouble. Well, if the Word assures us that we will be delivered from trouble, umm…I think that means that we will in fact have trouble. The assurance is that we will not have to stay in trouble.

IT promises us a Rescuer. And guess what, these promises apply to all types of troubles—those that were allowed and we had no control over as well as those we brought on ourselves. The promises of the Rescuer are not conditional on the source of the trouble. I have to tell you that when I mess up, it sure does feel good knowing that I have a guarantee of rescue, too. I won't be left in my mess.

IT says:

Exodus 14:14 NIV
The Lord will fight for you; you need only to be still.

Psalm 9:9-10 NIV
… [9]The LORD is a refuge for the oppressed, a stronghold in times of trouble. [10]Those who know your name trust in you, for you, LORD, have never forsaken those who seek you.

Psalm 34:19 NIV

*The righteous person may have **many** troubles, but **the** LORD delivers him from them all.*

Proverbs 12:13 NKJV

… But the righteous will come through trouble.

Matthew 21:21 NLT

You can even say to this mountain, 'May you be lifted up and thrown into the sea,' and it will happen.

Romans 5:3-5 NLT

[3] We can rejoice, too, when we run into problems and trials, for we know that they help us develop endurance. [4] And endurance develops strength of character, and character strengthens our confident hope of salvation. [5] And this hope will not lead to disappointment. For we know how dearly God loves us, because he has given us the Holy Spirit to fill our hearts with his love.

Romans 8:28 NIV

And we know that in all things God works for the good of those who love him, who have been called according to his purpose.

I realized the unforgiveness I was carrying wasn't hurting anyone but me... Forgiveness is not for the other person; it is for you!

Unforgiveness

I unknowingly lived many years with unforgiveness in my heart. You see, for the longest time, I equated forgiving the other person with giving them permission to keep hurting me. I grew up in a situation where I was constantly subjected to rejection, abandonment, and broken promises. I remember wanting to no longer interact with the person who was constantly hurting me but was repeatedly told, "you must forgive." So, I thought that I had no choice but to keep interacting with the person while taking whatever they dished out and chalking it up to life.

But what really happened was that I suppressed all that I felt about the situation and lived a "grin and bear it" life for many years. I built walls of protection and even went through a period of time where I didn't want to feel any emotions. I wanted no emotional attachment to anyone or anything. If someone was going to do the hurting, it was going to be me. I was not going to be the one hurt anymore. I knew I couldn't forgive if it meant that I still HAD to be involved with the person who hurt me.

But later in life, I realized the unforgiveness I was carrying wasn't hurting anyone but me. The person that I was angry at for the abuse and misuse had no clue why I was angry with them. They didn't even care that I was angry with them, and they blamed me for the anger that I felt. And the person

was still the same—breaking promises, rejecting me, and
unavailable—emotionally and physically.
Forgiveness is not for the other person; it is for you! It takes
the pressure off you and frees your heart from holding onto
any grudges or hurt that has been inflicted by another
person. Forgiveness does not mandate reunification with the
person; however, forgiveness is a mandate from God. As a
matter of fact, He promises that if we don't forgive others,
then He cannot forgive us.

IT says:

Matthew 18: 21-22 NIV
*Then Peter came to Jesus and asked, "Lord, how many
times shall I forgive my brother or sister who sins against
me? Up to seven times?" Jesus answered, "I tell you, not
seven times, but seventy-seven times.*

Mark 11:25 NLT
*But when you are praying, first forgive anyone you are
holding a grudge against, so that your Father in heaven
will forgive your sins, too."*

I was afraid to move forward, left, right or backwards—just too afraid of the next "land mine" that I may step on.

Unsafe/Uncertain

Have you ever been in a place in your life where you were just uncertain of everything? I know I have. It felt like one foot was on a banana peel and the other was in quicksand. During my wilderness experience, I felt like this more often than not. I was afraid to move forward, left, right or backwards—just too afraid of the next "land mine" that I may step on. It seemed that they were everywhere and there was just no stability in my life.

My safety net slowly became the Word of God. The more I saw Him be faithful to His Word, the more certain and balanced I became as I walked through life's twists, turns, and winding roads. His promise to cover me and to be a strong tower and a refuge for me strengthened my confidence in Him. His faithfulness became my place of stability. It became my safe place. It truly became my refuge.

My IT anchors during this time:

Psalm 2:12d NIV
Blessed are those who take refuge in Him…

Psalm 4:8 NIV
In peace I will lie down and sleep, for you alone, LORD, make me dwell in safety.

Psalm 12:6 NIV

And the words of the LORD are flawless…

Psalm 33:4 NIV

For the word of the Lord is right and true; he is faithful in all he does.

Psalm 91:4 NLT

He will cover you with his feathers. He will shelter you with his wings. His faithful promises are your armor and protection.

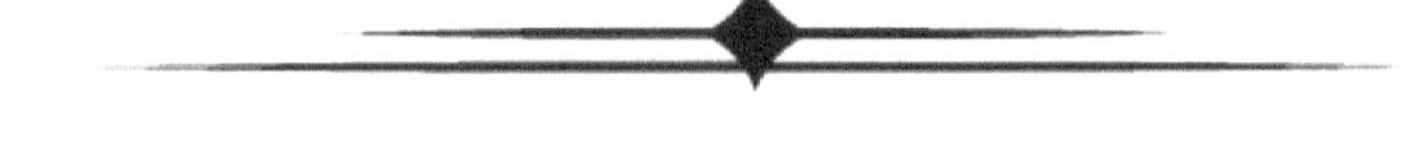

As tempting as it may be to clear our name or to vindicate ourselves,
it's not our place nor our right.

Vindication

I just want to get them back for the harm they have caused me and my family. I can't believe she lied about me like that. I have to confront him so that I can clear my name. Do they not know that I can destroy their reputation with the things I know about them?

Well, as tempting as it may be to clear our names or to vindicate ourselves, it's not our place, nor is it our right. Typically, when we try to do either of these, it becomes an even bigger mess. As Christians, our God promises to vindicate us. He promises to clear our name and "get them back" for us. We don't have to worry about our reputation or repaying a bad deed. Let God handle it. He knows better than anyone what repayment is most appropriate and effective. Guess what? He made these people, too. We are all His children, regardless of our actions towards each other.

What IT says:

Isaiah 54:17

NIV"...*no weapon forged against you will prevail, and you will refute every tongue that accuses you. This is the heritage of the servants of the* LORD, *and this is their vindication from me," declares the* LORD.

MSG...*but no weapon that can hurt you has ever been forged. Any accuser who takes you to court will be dismissed as a liar. This is what God's servants can*

expect. I'll see to it that everything works out for the best."
God's Decree.

2 Chronicles 20:15 NIV
*[15]He said: "Listen, King Jehoshaphat and all who live in Judah and Jerusalem! This is what the LORD says to you: 'Do not be afraid or discouraged because of **this** vast army. For the **battle** is **not yours**, but God's.*

Psalm 18:47 NLT
He is the God who pays back those who harm me;
he subdues the nations under me.

Psalm 35: 17-24 NIV
How long, Lord, will you look on? Rescue me from their ravages, my precious life from these lions. [18] I will give you thanks in the great assembly; among the throngs I will praise you.[19] Do not let those gloat over me who are my enemies without cause; do not let those who hate me without reason maliciously wink the eye. [20] They do not speak peaceably but devise false accusations against those who live quietly in the land. [21] They sneer at me and say, "Aha! Aha! With our own eyes we have seen it." [22] Lord, you have seen this; do not be silent. Do not be far from me, Lord. [23] Awake and rise to my defense! Contend for me, my God and Lord. [24] Vindicate me in your righteousness, Lord my God; do not let them gloat over me.

Remember,
nothing catches Him by surprise.

Walking Away from My Faith

I have to be totally honest here: I almost walked away from my faith. I stopped going to church. The mention of God made me grimace and hurt my heart. The very mention of His name angered me.

Why? I couldn't believe that the God that I served had allowed this series of blows in my life. I didn't want to tell anyone about this God of mine. How could I encourage anyone to follow Him? To believe in Him? To trust Him? "I did all of those things and look where it got me," is what I thought.

But His way had become such a vital part of me. No matter how hard I tried, I just couldn't totally let go forever. These are those times in life where we really have to remember and rely on just who God is, what His promises mean, and what He desires for us. This is when it's important to dig even deeper into IT to see what He has to say about our situations and for us to cling to His faithfulness.

One thing that I learned about myself during this wilderness experience was that I really did not know God or understand His nature. A lot of my understanding about Him was fragmented and misguided. I think in some ways, I treated God like a genie. I thought I could pray really hard to Him and He would trump my own will, which is such a contradiction to God's nature. Most times, He will allow us to do what we want—our will—even when He knows that our way is not best. He wants for us to follow Him and for His way to be our choice – not because He has forced us.

Also, during this season, there were times that I didn't have anything or anyone left to believe in or rely on but His word. As angry and disappointed as I was with Him and the outcome of my choices, I felt like I didn't have anywhere else to turn.

I had wished that I was dead. I even asked that He take me away from this life. I had contemplated taking my own life. I couldn't figure out how to just run away. (You know, throw my hands up and run in the opposite direction of my life while screaming to the top of my lungs!) I've often heard it said that when you're down to nothing, God is up to something. And He sure was! He was using this wilderness experience to reintroduce Himself to me; to show Me His strength, His faithfulness, His mercy, and His grace.

Remember, nothing catches Him by surprise.

His promises that got me through:

Psalm 22: 1-3; 7-11 NKJV

My God, My God, why have You forsaken Me? Why are You so far from helping Me, And from the words of My groaning? ² O My God, I cry in the daytime, but You do not hear; And in the night season, and am not silent. ³ But You are holy, …

*[7]All those who see Me ridicule Me; They shoot out the lip,
they shake the head, saying,
[8] "He trusted in the Lord, let Him rescue Him; Let Him
deliver Him, since He delights in Him!" [9]But You are He
who took Me out of the womb; You made Me trust while on
My mother's breasts. [10] I was cast upon You from birth.
From My mother's womb You have been My God. [11] Be not
far from Me, For trouble is near; For there is none to help.*

Proverbs 3:1-2; 5-6 NKJV

*My son, do not forget my law, But let your heart keep my
commands; [2] For length of days and long life And peace they will
add to you.
[5] Trust in the Lord with all your heart, And lean not on your
own understanding; [6] In all your ways acknowledge Him,
And He shall direct your paths.*

Joel 2:25 NLT

*The Lord says, "I will give you back what you lost to the
swarming locusts, the hopping locusts, the stripping
locusts, and the cutting locusts. It was I who sent this great
destroying army against you.*

Romans 8:28 NLT

*And we know that God causes everything to work together
for the good of those who love God and are called
according to his purpose for them.*

Wrapping IT Up

You see, I learned how to rest in the Lord during this wilderness season. The funny thing is that while my situations didn't always get better - in fact, sometimes they actually got worse - I got better. I matured. I learned how to rely on and trust of the faithfulness of my Almighty God. During my time in the wilderness, I gained a whole new perspective and understanding of the lyrics to of one of my favorite old hymns, *What A Friend We Have in Jesus:"*

"What a friend we have in Jesus, all our sins and griefs to bear! What a privilege to carry everything to God in prayer! Oh, what peace we often forfeit, Oh, what needless pain we bear…All because we do not carry everything to God in prayer!

Have we trials and temptations? Is there trouble anywhere? We should never be discouraged…Take it to the Lord in prayer. Can we find a friend so faithful, Who will all our sorrows share? Jesus knows our every weakness; Take it to the Lord in prayer.

What a friend we have in Jesus, all our sins and griefs to bear! What a privilege to carry everything to God in prayer! Oh, what peace we often forfeit, Oh, what needless pain we bear...All because we do not carry everything to God in prayer!

Are we weak and heavy-laden, cumbered with a load of care? Precious Savior, still our refuge...Take it to the Lord in

I was carrying so much on my shoulders and in my heart when I didn't have to. Our Mighty God is not only willing but also very capable of carrying the things that burden us. This is probably the most important lesson that I learned during my wilderness season: how to really let go and let God! For real! It is so much more than just a saying. He showed me how to navigate IT when I'm going through IT!

IT Finds Summary

Many times, when I was walking through my wilderness season I needed quick access to a scripture that I had read but couldn't remember where I read it. I kept thinking that it would be helpful to have the verses available in one easy and quick-to-access place. (Yes, I am assuming that you will keep this close and readily accessible to you. It's the best book you've ever read, right?) The following pages include the scripture references, their content, and the corresponding topics within this handbook.

I hope this helps!

Going Through?
Walk IT Out!

Scripture	Content	Topic
Psalm 139:14 NIV	I praise you because I am fearfully and wonderfully made; your works are wonderful, I know that full well	Acceptance
Romans 15:7 NIV	Accept one another, then, just as Christ accepted you, in order to bring praise to God.	Acceptance
Proverbs 19:11 NLT	Sensible people control their temper; they earn respect by overlooking wrongs.	Anger
Ephesians 4:26-27 NLT	[26] And "don't sin by letting anger control you."[a] Don't let the sun go down while you are still angry, [27] for anger gives a foothold to the devil.	Anger
James 1:19-20 NIV	[19] My dear brothers and sisters, take note of this: Everyone should be quick to listen, slow to speak and slow to become angry, [20] because human anger does not produce the righteousness that God desires.	Anger
Philippians 4:6 NIV	Do not be anxious about anything, but in every situation, by prayer and petition, with thanksgiving, present your requests to God.	Anxiety/ Worry
1 John 5: 14-15 NLT	[14] And we are confident that he hears us whenever we ask for anything that pleases him. [15] And since we know he hears us when we make our requests, we also know that he will give us what we ask for.	Anxiety/ Worry

Scripture	Content	Topic
Matthew 6:25-34 NIV	"Therefore I tell you, do not worry about your life, what you will eat or drink; or about your body, what you will wear. Is not life more than food, and the body more than clothes? [26] Look at the birds of the air; they do not sow or reap or store away in barns, and yet your heavenly Father feeds them. Are you not much more valuable than they? [27] Can any one of you by worrying add a single hour to your life[a]? [28] "And why do you worry about clothes? See how the flowers of the field grow. They do not labor or spin. [29] Yet I tell you that not even Solomon in all his splendor was dressed like one of these. [30] If that is how God clothes the grass of the field, which is here today and tomorrow is thrown into the fire, will he not much more clothe you—you of little faith? [31] So do not worry, saying, 'What shall we eat?' or 'What shall we drink?' or 'What shall we wear?' [32] For the pagans run after all these things, and your heavenly Father knows that you need them. [33] But seek first his kingdom and his righteousness, and all these things will be given to you as well. [34] Therefore do not worry about tomorrow, for tomorrow will worry about itself. Each day has enough trouble of its own.	Anxiety/ Worry

Scripture	Content	Topic
Proverbs 26: 27 NIV	Whoever digs a pit will fall into it; if someone rolls a stone, it will roll back on them.	Betrayal
Psalm 35:4-8 NIV	[4] May those who seek my life be disgraced and put to shame; may those who plot my ruin be turned back in dismay. [5] May they be like chaff before the wind, with the angel of the Lord driving them away;[6] may their path be dark and slippery, with the angel of the Lord pursuing them.	Betrayal
Psalm 34:18 NLT	The Lord is close to the brokenhearted; he rescues those whose spirits are crushed.	Brokenness
Proverbs 24:16 NIV	for though the righteous fall seven times, they rise again, but the wicked stumble when calamity strikes.	Brokenness
Romans 8:1-2 NIV	Therefore, there is now no condemnation for those who are in Christ Jesus, [2] because through Christ Jesus the law of the Spirit who gives life has set you[a] free from the law of sin and death.	Condemnation
John 10:27 KJV	My sheep hear my voice, and I know them, and they follow me...	Confusion
1 Corinthians 14:33 NKJV	For God is not the author of confusion, but of peace, as in all churches of the saints.	Confusion

Scripture	Content	Topic
2 Samuel 22:31 NIV and NLT	As for **God**, his way is perfect; the word of the LORD is perfect: He is a shield for all who look to him for protection.	Death of a Loved One
Psalm 30:5 NKJV	...Weeping may endure for a night, But joy *comes* in the morning.	Death of a Loved One
Psalm 34:18 NLT	The Lord is close to the brokenhearted; he rescues those whose spirits are crushed.	Death of a Loved One
Psalm 147:3 NLT	He heals the brokenhearted and bandages their wounds.	Death of a Loved One
2 Corinthians 5:6-8 NKJV	[6] So *we are* always confident, knowing that while we are at home in the body we are absent from the Lord. [7] For we walk by faith, not by sight. [8] We are confident, yes, well pleased rather to be absent from the body and to be present with the Lord.	Death of a Loved One
Romans 10: 9-10 NIV	[9] If you declare with your mouth, "Jesus is Lord," and believe in your heart that God raised him from the dead, you will be saved. [10] For it is with your heart that you believe and are justified, and it is with your mouth that you profess your faith and are saved.	Death of a Loved One-Salvation
Proverbs 13:12 NKJV	Hope deferred makes the heart sick, But *when* the desire comes, *it is* a tree of life.	Disappointment

Scripture	Content	Topic
Proverb 15:13 NIV	A happy heart makes the face cheerful, but heartache crushes the spirit.	Disappointment
Ex 14:14 NIV	The Lord will fight for me. I need only to be still.	Double-Mindedness
Proverbs 16:7 NKJV	When a man's ways please the LORD, he maketh even his enemies to be at peace with him.	Double-Mindedness
Proverbs 26:24-27 NIV	Enemies disguise themselves with their lips, but in their hearts they harbor deceit. [25] Though their speech is charming, do not believe them, for seven abominations fill their hearts. [26] Their malice may be concealed by deception, but their wickedness will be exposed in the assembly. [27] Whoever digs a pit will fall into it; if someone rolls a stone, it will roll back on them.	Double-Mindedness
Colossians 3:23 NKJV	Whatever you do, do your work heartily, as for the Lord rather than for men;	Double-Mindedness
James 1:8 KJV	A double minded man is unstable in all his ways.	Double-Mindedness
Joshua 1:9 NIV	Have I not commanded you? Be strong and courageous. Do not be afraid; do not be discouraged, for the Lord your God will be with you wherever you go."	Fear
Psalm 34:4 NIV	I sought the Lord, and he answered me; he delivered me from all my fears.	Fear

Scripture	Content	Topic
2 Timothy 1:7 KJV	For God hath not given us the spirit of fear; but of power, and of love, and of a sound mind.	Fear
Proverbs 3:5-6 NLT	Trust in the Lord with all your heart; do not depend on your own understanding. 6 Seek his will in all you do, and he will show you which path to take.	Fear
Isaiah 55: 8-9 NLT	"My thoughts are nothing like your thoughts," says the Lord. "And my ways are far beyond anything you could imagine. 9 For just as the heavens are higher than the earth, so my ways are higher than your ways and my thoughts higher than your thoughts.	Fear
Proverb 26:28 NIV	A lying tongue hates those it hurts, and a flattering mouth works ruin.	Flattery
Proverbs 29:5 NIV	Those who flatter their neighbors are spreading nets for their feet.	Flattery
Psalm 30:5 NKJV	Weeping may endure for a night, But joy *comes* in the morning.	Grief
Matthew 5:4 NIV	Blessed are those who mourn, for they will be comforted.	Grief
Romans 8:1 NIV	Therefore, there is now no condemnation for those who are in Christ Jesus,	Guilt/ Regret

Scripture	Content	Topic
Romans 8:1 MSG	[1-2] With the arrival of Jesus, the Messiah, that fateful dilemma is resolved. Those who enter into Christ's being-here-for-us no longer have to live under a continuous, low-lying black cloud. A new power is in operation. The Spirit of life in Christ, like a strong wind, has magnificently cleared the air, freeing you from a fated lifetime of brutal tyranny at the hands of sin and death.	Guilt/ Regret
Deuteronomy 31:6 NLT	Be strong and courageous. Do not be afraid or terrified because of them, for the Lord your God goes with you; he will never leave you nor forsake you."	I'm Alone/ Abandoned
Deuteronomy 31:8 NIV	The LORD himself goes before you and will be with you; he will never leave you nor forsake you. Do not be afraid; do not be discouraged."	I'm Alone/ Abandoned
Psalm 118:7a NIV	The Lord is with me; He is my helper.	I'm Alone/ Abandoned
2 Chronicles 16:9 ERV	*The eyes of the LORD go around looking in all the earth for people who are faithful to him so that he can make them strong.*	Overwhelmed
Psalm 14:2 NIV	The LORD looks down from heaven to see if there is anyone who is wise, anyone who looks to him for help.	Overwhelmed

Scripture	Content	Topic
Psalm 118:13 MSG	I was right on the cliff-edge, ready to fall, when God grabbed and held me.	Overwhelmed
Isaiah 54:17 NLT	But in that coming day no weapon turned against you will succeed. You will silence every voice raised up to accuse you. These benefits are enjoyed by the servants of the Lord; their vindication will come from me. I, the Lord, have spoken!	Revenge
Romans 12:19 KJV	Dearly beloved, avenge not yourselves, but rather give place unto wrath: for it is written, Vengeance is mine; I will repay, saith the Lord.	Revenge
Romans 12:19 NLT	Dear friends, never take revenge. Leave that to the righteous anger of God. For the Scriptures say, "I will take revenge; I will pay them back, says the Lord.	Revenge
Jeremiah 29:11 NIV	For I know the plans I have for you," declares the Lord, "plans to prosper you and not to harm you, plans to give you hope and a future.	Self-Harm Thoughts
Psalm 138:8 ESV	The Lord will fulfil his purpose, for me.	Self-Harm Thoughts
Psalm 139:16 NIV	Your eyes saw my unformed body; all the days ordained for me were written in your book before one of them came to be.	Self-Harm Thoughts

Scripture	Content	Topic
1 Corinthians 3:16-17 MSG	You realize, don't you, that you are the temple of God, and God himself is present in you? No one will get by with vandalizing God's temple, you can be sure of that. God's temple is sacred—and you, remember, *are* the temple.	Self-Harm Thoughts
Psalm 34:4-5 NIV	[4] I sought the Lord, and he answered me; he delivered me from all my fears. [5] Those who look to him are radiant; their faces are never covered with shame.	Shame
Romans 10:11 NKJV	[11] For the Scripture says, "Whoever believes on Him will not be put to shame."	Shame
Isaiah 53:5 NKJV	… and with his stripes we are healed.	Sickness
Psalm 91:3 NLT	For he will rescue you from every trap and protect you from deadly disease.	Sickness
Psalm 127: 2 NIV	In vain you rise early and stay up late, toiling for food to eat— for he grants sleep to those he loves.	Sleepless Nights
Proverbs 3:24 NIV	When you lie down, you will not be afraid; when you lie down, your sleep will be sweet.	Sleepless Nights
Exodus 14:14 NIV	The Lord will fight for you; you need only to be still.	Trouble/Trials/ Tribulations

Scripture	Content	Topic
Psalm 9:9-10 NIV	… [9]The LORD is a refuge for the oppressed, a stronghold in times of trouble. 10Those who know your name trust in you, for you, LORD, have never forsaken those who seek you.	Trouble/Trials/ Tribulations
Psalm 34:19 NIV	The righteous person may have **many** troubles, but **the** LORD delivers him from them all;	Trouble/Trials/ Tribulations
Proverbs 12:13 NKJV	… But the righteous will come through trouble.	Trouble/Trials/ Tribulations
Matthew 21:21 NLT	You can even say to this mountain, 'May you be lifted up and thrown into the sea,' and it will happen.	Trouble/Trials/ Tribulations
Romans 5:3-5 NLT	[3]We can rejoice, too, when we run into problems and trials, for we know that they help us develop endurance. [4]And endurance develops strength of character, and character strengthens our confident hope of salvation. [5]And this hope will not lead to disappointment. For we know how dearly God loves us, because he has given us the Holy Spirit to fill our hearts with his love.	Trouble/Trials/ Tribulations
Romans 8:28 NIV	And we know that in all things God works for the good of those who love him, who have been called according to his purpose.	Trouble/Trials/ Tribulations

Scripture	Content	Topic
Matthew 18: 21-22 NIV	Then Peter came to Jesus and asked, "Lord, how many times shall I forgive my brother or sister who sins against me? Up to seven times?" Jesus answered, "I tell you, not seven times, but seventy-seven times.	Unforgiveness
Mark 11:25 NLT	But when you are praying, first forgive anyone you are holding a grudge against, so that your Father in heaven will forgive your sins, too."	Unforgiveness
Psalm 2:12d NIV	Blessed are those who take refuge in Him	Unsafe/Uncertain
Psalm 4:8 NIV	In peace I will lie down and sleep, for you alone, LORD, make me dwell in safety.	Unsafe/Uncertain
Psalm 12:6 NIV	And the words of the Lord are flawless	Unsafe/Uncertain
Psalm 33:4 NIV	For the word of the Lord is right and true; he is faithful in all he does.	Unsafe/Uncertain
Psalm 91:4 NLT	He will cover you with his feathers. He will shelter you with his wings. His faithful promises are your armor and protection.	Unsafe/Uncertain

Scripture	Content	Topic
Isaiah 54:17 NIV Isaiah 54:17 MSG	"…no weapon forged against you will prevail, and you will refute every tongue that accuses you. This is the heritage of the servants of the Lord, and this is their vindication from me," declares the Lord….but no weapon that can hurt you has ever been forged. Any accuser who takes you to court will be dismissed as a liar. This is what God's servants can expect. I'll see to it that everything works out for the best." God's Decree.	Vindication
2 Chronicles 20:15 NIV	[15]He said: "Listen, King Jehoshaphat and all who live in Judah and Jerusalem! This is what the LORD says to you: 'Do not be afraid or discouraged because of this vast army. For the battle is not yours, but God's.	Vindication
Psalm 18:47 NLT	He is the God who pays back those who harm me; he subdues the nations under me.	Vindication

Scripture	Content	Topic
Psalm 35: 17-24 NIV	How long, Lord, will you look on? Rescue me from their ravages, my precious life from these lions. [18] I will give you thanks in the great assembly; among the throngs I will praise you. [19] Do not let those gloat over me who are my enemies without cause; do not let those who hate me without reason maliciously wink the eye. [20] They do not speak peaceably, but devise false accusations against those who live quietly in the land. [21] They sneer at me and say, "Aha! Aha! With our own eyes we have seen it." [22] Lord, you have seen this; do not be silent. Do not be far from me, Lord. [23] Awake, and rise to my defense! Contend for me, my God and Lord. [24] Vindicate me in your righteousness, Lord my God; do not let them gloat over me.	Vindication
Romans 8:28 NLT	And we know that God causes everything to work together for the good of those who love God and are called according to his purpose for them.	Walking Away from My Faith

Scripture	Content	Topic
Proverbs 3:1-2; 5-6 NKJV	My son, do not forget my law, But let your heart keep my commands; 2 For length of days and long life And peace they will add to you. 5 Trust in the Lord with all your heart, And lean not on your own understanding; 6 In all your ways acknowledge Him, And He shall direct your paths.	Walking Away from My Faith
Joel 2:25 NLT	The Lord says, "I will give you back what you lost to the swarming locusts, the hopping locusts, the stripping locusts, and the cutting locusts. It was I who sent this great destroying army against you.	Walking Away from My Faith
Psalm 22: 1-3; 7-11 NKJV	My God, My God, why have You forsaken Me? *Why are You so* far from helping Me, *And from* the words of My groaning? 2 O My God, I cry in the daytime, but You do not hear; And in the night season, and am not silent. 3 But You *are* holy,… 7All those who see Me ridicule Me; They shoot out the lip, they shake the head, *saying,* 8 "He trusted in the Lord, let Him rescue Him; Let Him deliver Him, since He delights in Him!" 9But You *are* He who took Me out of the womb; You made Me trust *while* on My mother's breasts. 10 I was cast upon You from birth. From My mother's womb You *have been* My God. 11 Be not far from Me, For trouble *is* near; For *there is* none to help.	Walking Away from My Faith

About The Author

B. C. Raines describes herself as a recovering sinner. She knows that she is saved but admits that she still makes mistakes, even sometimes repeating the same mistake over and over again. It is from this place of transparency, honesty, and vulnerability that she encourages others (especially her sisters in Christ) to have faith because we have a Savior who loves us unconditionally. She is a woman of God, anointed to help (minister to) others.

She is a mother, daughter, sister, aunt, and friend who is passionate about encouraging others to be their best selves - in spite of the adverse situations they may face. She shares her personal life struggles in an effort to inspire others to keep stepping up to the next level in life.

B.C. Raines is also the founder of Sister U Matter!® a self-discovery movement and awareness campaign inspired by her first published book, *I Am The Crown*. She is a contributing author to *The Women of New Life and is* the founder of SUM! Unlimited, the nonprofit extension of Sister U Matter! LLC.

Additional Resources

The following pages include national hotline numbers and resources that are available when you may be experiencing some of the emotions or situations that I have talked about in this handbook. If you need a safe place to talk or just some helpful hints to consider, check out these additional resources.

National Hotline Resources

Domestic Violence	National Domestic Violence Hotline 24/7	1-800-799 -7233
Food Assistance	USDA National Hunger Hotline 7:00 AM – 10:00 PM Eastern Time	1-866-3-HUNGRY or 1-877-8-HAMBRE
Mental Health Awareness	SAMHSA's National Helpline 24/7	1-800-662-HELP (4357) TTY: 1-800-487-4889
Crisis, Grief Resources	National Crisis Hotline	1-800-273-8255
Sexual Assault	National Sexual Assault Hotline 24/7	1-800-656-4673
Suicide Emergency Response	Emergency response 24/7	911
Suicide Prevention	988 Suicide and Crisis Lifeline 24/7	988

Depression Tips

Shower. Not a bath, a shower. Use water as hot or cold as you like. You don't even need to wash. Just get in under the water and let it run over you for a while. Sit on the floor if you must.

Moisturize everything. Use whatever lotion you like. Unscented? Dollar store lotion? Fancy 48-hour lotion that makes you smell like a field of wildflowers? Use whatever you want and use it all over your entire dermis.

Get dressed. Put on clean, comfortable clothes.

Put on your favorite underwear. Cute black lacy panties? Those ridiculous boxers you bought last Christmas with candy cane hearts on the butt? Put them on.

Drink cold water. Use ice. If you want, add some mint or lemon for an extra boost.

Clean something. Doesn't have to be anything big. Organize one drawer of a desk. Wash five dirty dishes. Do a load of laundry. Scrub the bathroom sink.

Blast music. Listen to something upbeat and dancey and loud, something that's got lots of energy. Sing to it, dance to it, even if you suck at both.

Make food. Don't just grab a granola bar to munch. Take the time and make food. Even if it's ramen. Add something special to it, like a soft-boiled egg or some veggies. Prepare food, it tastes way better, and you'll feel like you accomplished something.

Make something. Write a short story or a poem, draw a picture, color a picture, fold origami, crochet or knit, sculpt something out of clay, anything artistic. Even if you don't think you're good at it. Create.

Go outside. Take a walk. Sit in the grass. Look at the clouds. Smell flowers. Put your hands in the dirt and feel the soil against your skin.

Call someone. Call a loved one, a friend, a family member, call a chat service if you have no one else to call. Talk to a stranger on the street. Have a conversation and listen to someone's voice. If you can't bring yourself to call, text or email or whatever, just have some social interaction with another person. Even if you don't say much, listen to them. It helps.

Cuddle your pets. Cuddle your pets if you have them/can cuddle them. Take pictures of them. Talk to them. Tell them how you feel, about your favorite movie, a new game coming out, anything.

May seem small or silly to some, but this list keeps people alive.

*** At your absolute best you won't be good enough for the wrong people. But at your worst, you'll still be worth it to the right ones. Remember that. Keep holding on.

*** In case nobody has told you today, I love you and you are worth your weight and then some in gold, so be kind to yourself and most of all keep pushing on!!!!

Find something to be grateful for!

Author Unknown

Possible Signs of Intimate Partner Violence (Domestic Violence)

Abusive relationships always involve an imbalance of power and control. An abuser uses intimidating, hurtful words and behaviors to control a partner.

It might not be easy to identify domestic violence at first. While some relationships are clearly abusive from the outset, abuse often starts subtly and gets worse over time.

You might be experiencing domestic violence if you're in a relationship with someone who:

- Calls you names, insults you or puts you down.

- Prevents or discourages you from going to work or school or seeing family members or friends.

- Tries to control how you spend money, where you go, what medicines you take or what you wear.

- Acts jealous or possessive or constantly accuses you of being unfaithful.

- Gets angry when drinking alcohol or using drugs.

- Threatens you with violence or a weapon.

- Hits, kicks, shoves, slaps, chokes or otherwise hurts you, your children or your pets.

- Forces you to have sex or engage in sexual acts against your will.

- Blames you for his or her violent behavior or tells you that you deserve it.

If you're in a same-sex relationship or if you're bisexual or transgender, you might also be experiencing abuse if you're in a relationship with someone who:

- Threatens to tell friends, family, colleagues or community members your sexual orientation or gender identity.

- Tells you that authorities won't help you because of your sexuality or gender identity.

- Justifies abuse by questioning your sexuality or gender identity.

Source: Domestic violence against women: Recognize patterns, seek help - Mayo Clinic

Going Through?
Walk IT Out!